Diggin' For Refuge:
Miles of Grace & Transition

Arlecia Simmons

Diggin' for Refuge:
Miles of Grace & Transition
Copyright © 2022 by Arlecia Simmons

Cover Illustration:
Martina Wilson, AYM Advertising

Ordering Information:
Quantity sales. Special discounts are available on quantity purchases by corporations, associations, and others. For details, contact the publisher, admin@drlecia.com. Orders by U.S. trade bookstores and wholesalers. Please visit https://drlecia.com/
Printed in the United States of America

Table of Contents

DEDICATION

To all who provided refuge through housing, meals, love gifts, laughter, prayer, book purchases, transportation, celebrations, preaching invitations, and the ministry of presence from February to August 2017.

"I cried unto thee, O Lord: I said, Thou art my refuge and my portion in the land of the living."
Psalm 142:5 (KJV)

PREFACE

No one prepares for life to come unraveled in a matter of days or weeks. If you've ever been divorced, experienced a sudden layoff, or had a healthy relative quickly develop an illness and die, then you, too, have experienced how life can come at you fast. And when I say quick, I mean faster than an IRS payment on Autopay. There are some seasons in life where we are prepared for the space we are navigating, and then there are seasons where we end up asking, *"God, how did we end up here?"* There is silence instead of hearing God's voice in prayer and meditation. COMPLETE SILENCE. Roaches even stop walking.

Not only is there silence, but it feels like the ground beneath you is porous, shaky, and crumbling. *Transitions* are moments or seasons when you can't talk about having faith, but the word must become flesh as you *"...walk through the valley of the shadow of death "* (Psalm 23: 4).

As Jesus says in the Sermon on the Mount in Matthew 5:45, *"it rains on the just and the unjust."* In a matter of a week, I went from being the pastor of a church that sat on nearly three acres of land in Washington, D.C., to packing all of my belongings in a storage unit in rural

Maryland. "Y'all got mice around here?" I asked before signing the contract for who knew how many months.

I had packed up all my earthly possessions and didn't have much of a plan beyond taking a course in transitional ministry and returning to the five-fold ministry as an evangelist. Honestly, I needed a break from shepherding God's people, and I needed to hear *good news* for my soul.

I had one month of salary left, faith in God, and frustration as I sought to understand if this current situation would result in a blessing or curse. As I dug for refuge from February to August 2017 or participated in what is referred to as *couch surfing*, I found gifts wrapped in unexpected packages and extended in unforeseen ways.

This book isn't a fictional read. It's a manuscript of transparency because truth-telling is my superpower. I share my truth in hopes others will be strengthened even as they confront their gritty truths, prepare for transitions, and navigate existing ones that reveal God's grace in unanticipated ways. As you read, you will likely have many questions about the choices made, but keep in mind that hindsight is 20-20, and often the obvious isn't as apparent when navigating crises. Often, survival is the primary goal.

Resignation Letter

January 18, 2017

Dear Moderator ... and Members:

During the past 18 months, God has been gracious unto us as we have journeyed together in the covenant relationship of pastor and congregation. We have experienced God's faithfulness as we strived to further the mission of Faith United Church of Christ.

After much prayer, reflection, and counsel, I am writing to notify you of my resignation. My last day as pastor of Faith United Church of Christ will be Friday, March 31, 2017. I will be returning to my evangelistic ministry.

While our time together has not been without struggle, all of us are better because of the lessons learned and how God stretched us as we created new programming, enhanced worship, and moved #FaithForward.

I thank you for allowing me to be your pastor and for what you have risked and sacrificed during this season. During the next few weeks, I look forward to doing whatever is needed to ease the transition.

Sincerely,

Rev. Arlecia D. Simmons, Ph.D., M.Div.

INTRODUCTION

Transition is nothing new to me. I have experienced many as an adult, but I had a reasonably stable childhood with minimal movement, unlike others I know. Before age 18, I had only moved once in my entire life. For many, that's rare. I once worked with a sister who laughed at me when I couldn't get settled in an academic institution where we worked. My office was painted the first week of the school year, so I sat in the hall trying to make sense of my new schedule as an assistant professor. Having just moved to the city two days before school, I sought normalcy and ease that didn't exist. Oh, and did I mention I moved to another state only a day before the start of school? If it wasn't one thing, it was another, and it seems like I couldn't get settled in the office where dead cockroaches stared at me with a heavenly gaze as I looked up at my fluorescent light each day.

During one of those first few days during a casual conversation in the hallway, a colleague I quickly connected with finally broke it down for me why it didn't bother her not to have an office as an adjunct professor.

"I don't even have childhood pictures," she said. Because her ministry entrenched

family was poor and often short on rent, she recalled a childhood of late-night escapes to other locations before the rent was due. There were no memories of favorite blankets or toys she had kept since childhood. Her formative years were framed by a mixture of lots of church and lots of transition. That was not my story, and there was always the desire to settle quickly when arriving in a new space because I had memories to unpack.

As an educator, I've encountered children who may have attended three to four schools during a school year while I attended my grandmother's same school, which was also the same school my mother and her four siblings attended. At the time of this writing, my 93-year-old grandmother had only three mailing addresses during her entire adulthood. Thus, all the "mixing up" I have done has never entirely made sense to her. However, she and my deceased grandfather still prayed and supported me along the way. When I drove from Iowa to North Carolina, she sat in her recliner the entirety of my travels and refused to leave the phone over the two days.

At age 11, my mother moved us out of my grandparents' home, the only home I had known, to an apartment complex a few miles away. After high school, I moved away to college. Three weeks after graduating, I made my first adult move to Eden, N.C.

As the writer of the Gospel of John suggested in John 21:25, there wouldn't be room for all of what I call my "dummy missions," foolery, and shenanigans. Although many of the physical moves were challenging and came with costly life lessons and the blessing of extended family members, I learned with each of them that God's grace was present everywhere my feet tread, even if I found myself with a broken toe or bruised heel.

Nearly ten years later, God showed amazing grace when I moved to Iowa City, Iowa, where someone from South Carolina told me they had no trees, and it was always cold. I gave away most of my wardrobe before leaving South Carolina, thinking I would always require a fleece coat. I left for Iowa in August and found many trees, ended up with a heat rash, and chafe thighs due to the new jeans-only wardrobe I had initially taken. You see, you can't take everyone's advice when preparing for a transition as those who have never taken the journey can only speculate about the itinerary and things to pack.

The moves before 2017 were often strategic and usually planned out. Well, not all of them, but that's another book. The transitions before this time were for new jobs or educational opportunities, so they were planned activities and goals on the other side. While I never saw anything unusual about being non-military personnel exploring the world, others always questioned my moves. "What is she doing now?" they would ask my mom or relatives but wouldn't dare ask me or lend a hand in any of the moves.

My times of transition in adulthood have included:

North Charleston, S.C. to Eden, N.C., to Sumter, S.C. to Ladson, S.C. to Columbia S.C., to Charlotte, N.C., to Orangeburg, S.C., to Iowa City, Iowa to Durham, N.C., to Augusta, GA., to Columbia, S.C., to the

DMV, which was the last stop before the events of this book took place. I've had everyone move me from classmates, church folks, and even former lovers. This time around was much different, and there was no immediate destination.

In January 2017, on the observance of the Martin Luther King, Jr. holiday, I was invited and paid to come and empower women attending a 60th birthday party in Washington, D.C. Initially, it felt like a strange request. I soon learned that D.C. was a different kind of place where people booked speakers for birthday and Christmas parties. It took a minute for me to understand what the guest of honor wanted to accomplish that evening. I finally figured it out, and we agreed on an acceptable honorarium.

After I spoke, encouraged, and prayed, I went and sat at the dining room table where the exquisite birthday cake was being cut. It was a grand dessert with layers and layers of flavor and cold and room temperature ingredients. The host explained more about this cake as I sat at the table where I was introduced to one of the birthday girl's friends who didn't take long to speak into my life with a Word of Knowledge. "You're about to shift and move," said this stranger as I savored the birthday cake. I had never seen or spoken to this woman before, but she knew that my life was about to change in only a few days. My resignation letter had been written, and it would soon be sent out to every member, per denominational requirements for separating with a congregation.

CHAPTER ONE
BEFORE I LET GO

Why did he place my pots in a plastic bag?" I mumbled in frustration as I returned to my Silver Spring apartment after visiting my storage unit. Half of my cooking pots were left in the apartment after my final trip to the storage unit in Burtonsville, Md. I don't even want to talk about the "he," who I had to invite back into my life after a short-lived "ship" that was more pain than joy. (*I wrote about this "he" in chapter nine of Diggin' For Intimacy: Sex, Sensuality, and Loving God," the second book in the series*). "He" was the only person I had to assist me as I tried to finish cleaning a three-bedroom, two-bath apartment I had only spent seven months in after living in the death trap of a townhouse a few miles down the road.

The three-bedroom townhouse that was my only option in August 2016 was wedged between two families with children, and it was the only place I could afford as I attempted to do the Lord's work. My first townhouse in the DMV was infested with mice, and an allergy test conducted after ongoing respiratory infections found mice urine in my antibodies.

While I didn't realize it was possible, I believe I developed PTSD after months of exterminator visits for a matter that wouldn't go away until I relocated to this apartment that added 15 minutes to my commute. An additional quarter of an hour driving in the DMV isn't what you want in your life when you're from the South and haven't practiced with NASCAR. Before moving to the DMV, I realized housing would be a challenge due to the amount of money allotted for my pastoral allowance and the housing costs in the area, which are among the highest in the United States. Before moving, a friend who worked for the federal government and lived in D.C. suggested I consider living in a convent with nuns, which was realistically a short-term possibility. My friend, who lived in D.C. for years and was a presidential appointee, knew of others who had done the same, and I trusted her opinion. However, members of the congregation responsible for my transition didn't think that was the best option. A realtor, who assisted me because of her friendship with a church member, graciously helped me find the apartment that neither of us realized would be a nightmare.

Now both housing experiences were behind me, and I was yet again trying to find refuge somewhere. The thought of lodging at a convent returned, and I called a group of nuns in Maryland in early February 2017. Still, God had another plan as February ended, and I began moving out of "Crunkville."

The Sunday before moving day, a Service of Release followed the 11 a.m. worship service on Sunday, February 26, 2017. Along with family, friends, and visiting clergy, the congregation ended the day at a reception that featured a strawberry shortcake I had mentioned to a deacon that I had enjoyed. I took pictures of the happenings, and we exchanged our final pleasantries.

As I closed my office door and left the premises, my girlfriends escorted me to my car. A friend of 25 years, a sister I met in Orangeburg, S.C., 15 years earlier, one of my Iowa Sista Docs, and a new friend made in D.C. walked alongside me. A clergy sister standing in the parking lot noted the powerful imagery of that moment. These friends refused to leave me alone, and although I didn't realize it, their presence was escorting me into an unknown spirit where I would need the power of God and the presence of my ancestors.

After throwing away a dozen white roses gifted to me by the female clergy of my denomination because I had nowhere to put them, I took my iron frying pan and remaining kitchen items to the dumpster before dropping off my helper-outer.

I offered the roses to the office attendant charged with checking my unit and retrieving my keys, but she didn't want them. I wanted someone to enjoy them, but

I could not hold on to them like so many things I had to discard. It was time to go.

I gave my helper-outer a few dollars, dropped him off at a nearby bus stop, turned in my keys after a final walk-thru, and spent more than an hour trying to find a box to ship my cable elements back before driving to Washington, D.C., from Silver Spring. Thankfully, a church visitor who later became a friend offered to let me stay with her for a few days before I would begin my adventures of "Girl, Where Are You Going?" On that gloomy day, it felt like I was auditioning for a new season of "Punked" because it was one challenge after another, including the store attendant trying to sell me a cardboard box for $10 to ship the cable box back when they had a contract with the cable company. He finally accepted the cable elements when he saw I wasn't giving up the duckies and gave me a receipt.

Within 48 hours, I went from Senior Pastor of a "church on the hill" to a four-degree-having 42-year-old whose life felt like it was slowly about to unravel. The only thing that I knew for sure was that I had feet. And I was shaking the dust off them to walk into a new beginning that did not come with an itinerary.

I had a laundry list of things I needed in the days and months to come.

- Employment
- Money to pay bills
- An endorsement for the continued recognition of my ordination
- Health Insurance
- Sinus medication
- Car note payments
- Housing
- A reminder of my purpose in life
- Courage

This list was not exhaustive, and I didn't have six – or nine months' worth of savings as advised by financial advisors. The only thing I had was faith, but even that was wavering. What kind of God would allow a daughter to experience such a great accomplishment 21 months earlier only to drop her headfirst and then tell her to walk and live?

While my health and self-esteem were both in shambles, the one thing that was left untouched was a half of a mustard seed of faith in a God who had seen me through difficult seasons before. However, this time around was different, and half of my mustard seed was crushed and, in a bag, called "first pastoral ministry."

After a process that began in October 2013 when I submitted my ministerial resume via e-mail to June 2015 when the congregation voted to call me as a pastor, I had wondered where God was at work in me and this process. The process also included the congregation I finally served, initially choosing another candidate in May 2014, and then calling me back to become a candidate again in February 2015. Months earlier, I was notified that I was a finalist of another congregation in Montgomery, Ala. But things didn't feel right during the selection process, so I removed myself from candidacy. You know there's something about listening to that still small voice or nudge that speaks to you. I'm not sure if I always trusted my discernment throughout the pastoral search process that started in 2012 when I was preparing to graduate from Duke Divinity School. Often, I did, but I often second-guessed if it was God, me, or fear speaking.

After you've experienced grace, you get a hint of what it feels like as God makes a way when there is no way. There are songs, scripture, and folk sayings that don't make sense to us until we've lived long enough for the word to become flesh and frame our emotions and physical state. But how did I end up in a state I had only read or written about but never actually lived? While I have written about the plight of the homeless as a former daily newspaper reporter, I don't believe I've ever interviewed someone actively homeless. I do recall interviewing people who had experienced housing security. Still, I don't remember asking any about their day-to-day experience trying to figure out where they would lay their heads. So often, we envision homelessness as the veteran who never mentally returned home after Vietnam, so now, he roams the streets asking if she can do odd jobs for food or change. Or maybe the face of homelessness has become the female addict who exchanges her body for alcohol and drugs? The face of homelessness or housing insecurity could be the face you see behind a mask at the grocery store or on a socially distanced pew in church.

While my parents prefer I not use the word "homeless" to describe the period I will describe here, it's the only word that makes sense to me for those months of wilderness wandering from state to state, city to city, and guest room to guest room. Unlike others who find shelter under bridges and on streets across the globe, I had a 2016 Toyota Corolla that I purchased only months earlier and the hospitality of people I had met through employment, education, ministry, and life. "Five Months of Grace" is what I named the season that transpired after I left my position as senior pastor in Washington, D.C. I was not fired, and my contract was not up, but my time had expired as the leader of this flock. The start of 2017 required a new beginning outside of a pulpit.

While I could write an entire book on the backstory that led to my departure 21 months into my pastorate, I've found that the story that will edify the Body of Christ is the one that is birthed after that assignment. Although it was a decision saturated in prayer, spiritual and therapeutic spiritual counsel, it was still difficult and not desired. In life, uncomfortable and unpopular decisions must be made.

During the global coronavirus pandemic, we have read and learned more about a phenomenon called "the Great Resignation," where workers from various industries have left the workforce because of the stress of the virus, and other lingering reasons were amplified during the pandemic. As I read the media accounts, I understood the plights of the named and unnamed who told their stories about knowing when to leave their hourly and salaried positions. Sometimes during a transition, you know where you want to go, and other times you only know it's time to move forward, even if you're not sure where you are going.

When it's time to go, it's time to go. For me, it was time to trust the God I had preached about and told the people in the pews to trust.

Refuge Reflection

In recent years, I decided that my health care team needed to be made up of women of color. While serving in the DMV, my medical providers included an African-American female physician originally from Georgia supported by a physician assistant of Asian descent. These two women and a handful of specialists made up my dream team of providers.

I needed TOUGH love and strong talk, and not another prescription for areas of health that I can control by behavior modification. The Georgia peach, who was my primary care physician, didn't always come with sweet words as she provided care to me and likely the other female senior pastors she often noted caring for because our symptoms and excuses were often similar.

During a bi-annual exam in December 2016, she diagnosed me with having depression and "jacked me up" about choosing to live or continuing my vocation! I was like, "Is she holding me accountable and making me cry in this office?" It was needed. I wasn't just her patient, but I felt she saw me as a sister she didn't want to self-destruct. I had never had a physician caring for my physical body diagnose me with depression until this time. I was grateful for this holistic care as our bodies often manifest and "carry the score" of what is happening within us emotionally.

While I usually saw the physician's assistant who spent months trying to figure out why I was dealing with a reoccurring digestive issue that was finally attributed to stress, the doctor was only confirming what I already knew and had discussed with the therapists and ministry coach I had been consulting with along the way. My blood pressure had become more elevated, but we started attributing it to rushing in from traffic or some other environmental factor that may have influenced that day's reading. I had found myself in a perfect storm, and by this time on the journey, I could respond that the winds were soon about to die down because I was preparing to resign within the next six weeks.

However, would the flooding that often comes with storms take me out in the interim?

During that late evening appointment, I told the doctor that there was a plan in place, and I was preparing to take the needed steps to help save my life. By this time on the journey, news media had started to report that various pastors in the United States were taking their lives through suicide. While news organizations traditionally do not report on incidents of suicide, pastors are often considered "public figures" in their communities. These stories spread as national media have picked up the reports that are shared digitally and amplified a once silenced issue: pastors were in distress.

Before the pandemic, pastors leaving the pulpit have been an area of concern and research interest. Still, it's an area that's not as amplified until a clergy person commits suicide or does something tragically that becomes a major news story. Having read the stories and research published on the matter, I knew taking my life to end the troubling season wasn't the path I wanted to take. Most of the clergy suicides reported have been the stories of male clergy, yet female clergy are more silently dealing with the stressors while some seek out safe sanctuaries in closed Facebook groups.

In December 2016, Pepperdine University and the Barna Group announced the release of a landmark study titled, *The State of Pastors*, which drew from interviews with more than 10,000 pastors from 40 denominations across all 50 states. Startling data was revealed as the report discussed the burnout of pastors. As a black Baptist, there was minimal talk about women in ministry and minimal discussion about burnouts, sabbaticals, healthy boundaries, and rest beyond the annual month-long vacation that included a week at a denominational conference.

Barna researchers and other organizations highlight self-care and mental health maintenance among clergy. During my tenure as pastor, I recall participating in a similar study that sought to gauge the wellness of senior pastors. It was a phone interview, and I remember being contacted on one of my gloomiest days. I wish I had paid more attention to the group conducting that study.

During the Covid-19 pandemic in 2021, a Barna poll found that nearly two in five pastors had considered quitting full-time ministry. The same survey noted that 46 percent of pastors under 45 reported considering leaving full-time ministry, compared to 34 percent of pastors 45 and older. I was 43 years old when I submitted my resignation letter.

The State of Pastors and additional reports can be accessed at Barna.com.

March 26, 2017, Facebook Post

In January, as the nation received its 45th president, members of my congregation were notified that I had resigned as senior pastor.

On Sunday, February 26, I preached my final sermon at [the church I pastored]. My father's aunt came to represent my family and held me close as the Conference Minister prayed over the congregation and me.

A Service of Release followed the 11 a.m. worship service, and the congregation, family, friends, and visiting clergy ended the day at a reception. As I closed my office door and left the premises, my girlfriends escorted me to my car. A friend of 25 years, a sister I met in Orangeburg 15 years ago, one of my Iowa Sista Docs, and a new friend made in DC walked alongside me. A clergy sister standing in the parking lot noted the powerful imagery of that moment.

I am grateful for the opportunity to have served "the church on the hill" for nearly two years. I learned so much about myself, learned from other colleagues, and tapped into more spiritual gifts that had not manifested before! There's healing in my hands.

I am grateful to all who prayed for me from a distance or popped in to visit. God always sent familiar faces when I needed to see them the most. Those visits reminded the congregation how beloved I was on the earth as former students, classmates, and colleagues coordinated their travels to worship with us!

I am grateful for my parents, family, friends, and mentors who supported my decision. In the words of the Apostle Paul, "I am certain that God, who began the good work in [me], will continue his work until it is finally finished on the day when Christ Jesus returns."

God is a "Divine yoga instructor" who uses assignments to stretch us beyond what we could ask or think. Who else could take you almost 600 miles away from home to a city you have only visited as a tourist to pastor for the very first time, a church in a denomination that you knew little about beyond one congregation in Chicago that you stream online? Oh, yeah, as a single woman.

When you take the limits off God, God will take limits off of you! I was able to plant *and water, and I am convinced God and the community will get the increase!*

Ministry didn't end on February 26, which was Transfiguration Sunday, but it continues as I remain faithful to this wondrous calling!

*I continue to **#looknlive** and walk by faith and not by sight!*

CHAPTER TWO
WHO CAN I RUN TO?

On March 2, 2017, I woke up in a friend's master bedroom while she slept on an air mattress in her home gym. After the stress of packing and entering a transition, she recognized I needed comfort and rest. This was sacrificial then and even now as I think about the concept of sisterhood and the call to bear one another's burdens.

If you only have good friends when everything is going well, you need new friends! The first week and a half after packing up, I found refuge with two friends living in D.C. While I had events to attend in

North Carolina scheduled, it wasn't time to move yet. I needed to get my mind right before I headed to North Carolina to attend a ministerial conference at Shaw Divinity School and a clergywomen gathering at the Franklinton Center at Bricks in Whitakers, N.C. The latter would be a meeting filled with women pastors and ministers in the denomination I served, and many of them knew of my departure while others would soon learn during our gathering.

This national gathering of female ministers would be enjoyable as I navigated a new role with no sought-after title and no glowing details to provide about my next steps. Thankfully, the women welcomed me during my new journey, and I enjoyed the fellowship, worship, and God knows I enjoyed the food. The meals were cooked by some country folks who had journeyed to the site to prepare home-cooked meals daily. When you're on the move, you value meals that aren't coming out of styrofoam boxes and paper bags. As a foodie, the daily meals, ministered to my weary soul.

Out of Order Comedy Birthed

It's often after complicated pregnancies that many realize the amount of grace needed to birth babies whose lives were hanging in the balance as they wrestled to get from womb to bosom. During this challenging season of rebirth, God began to birth a not-so-hidden talent that only family, friends, and social media followers had experienced in posts.

Amid all the chaos and uncertainty, God started giving me jokes to tell. For years, I had written notes or funnies. Still, it wasn't until I began preparing to transition out of my pastorate that I started dedicating minutes here-and-there to craft sketches to become material that I hoped to perform one day. *Google Docs* is a godsend for having a space you can use to dump the craziness and creativity in your brain.

While talking with one of my ministerial mentors, Pastor Cheryl Moore Adamson, about her upcoming women's conference held in Myrtle Beach in mid-March, she mentioned finalizing plans for their annual women's conference. She asked me if I wanted to put together a comedy routine! Thus, the birth of the *Out of Order Comedy Experience.*

I was what they called "free 'til I was fool," and I didn't have to prove anything to anyone. I was broken. I packaged those little pieces up and wrote a 40-minute comedy routine and a sermon I would preach the next day.

Would they laugh? Will they get my sense of humor? Are these jokes a little too raunchy? Most of the jokes I wrote were about body transitions in midlife, relationships, and some of the content was a tad edgy. If these jokes didn't work with the church ladies, I'm sure they could work for a crowd sucking on chicken wings and sipping on gin and juice.

But what does a comedienne wear? What look was I going for? I mean, if I was going to make a fool of myself, then I needed to look good doing it, or why bother?

One day while waiting for my car to be serviced in Rock Hill, S.C., I walked over to the mall where I found one of those cheesy spray paint t-shirt kiosks. Impressed with the artist's work, I told her I needed a tee that incorporated a butterfly, and it needed to read "Look 'N Live Ministries" and

"Doctah Lele," a name I had started to use online after being given the moniker by a Duke Divinity School classmate.

We agreed on a price, and I went and grabbed a fish sandwich as she created my "wardrobe" for my first official comedy show. Weeks later, with my new tee and a new pair of jeans I had purchased before leaving the DMV, I performed my first show in a Myrtle Beach resort conference room. Scared that I would bomb, I asked that it not be recorded, which was one of the biggest mistakes I could make. I was a hit among the women gathered. I was proud of myself but was too afraid to have digital receipts.

The women laughed, teared up, participated in call and response, and affirmed my gift of storytelling and what I later called the "Joy Ministry." As that session concluded and the women walked to their game night activity, I was blessed to hear conversations about issues I had previously made them laugh about. The younger and older women discussed expectations in marriage, including sex, which is rarely discussed in such settings. "They won't listen to me," said a woman who sat quietly during most of the sessions, as she referenced something I said about the older women helping prepare us for body changes and relationships.

As I reflected on that almost forty minutes of making attendees laugh, I realized that evoking laughter was a ministry in itself. I was doing what I had always done but via a different medium. The Bible tells us, *"Laughter is like medicine,"* so I was blessed that I could share a balm with others. One that my soul needed.

After leaving the retreat in Myrtle Beach and staying in Conway another night with the convener's mother, I journeyed to a resort on Pawley's Island, a coastal location between Myrtle Beach and Charleston. The two-night stay that I booked on *Groupon* was in a room that wasn't as palatial as the beach resort I had just left, and it was a distance from the water.

The room with dated furniture and a scratchy, cheap polyester comforter, along with the "Beware of Alligators" posters near the elevator, made me wonder if this is what my future looked like. Was this experience going to eat me alive, or would I live to have a testimony of beauty from ashes?

The only thing missing was an ashtray filled with cigarette butts and a blinking light outside. Later, someone familiar with the resort told me I was staying in the basic quarters of this site, so I'll have to upgrade my life to get to experience what I hadn't via this Groupon offer. While I had brought a plate of vittles with me from my favorite soul food buffet in Conway, I had to locate food eventually.

I ventured out and found a locally owned restaurant that had some collard green egg rolls and some other fare that held me over! The winds were blowing hard, and the chill in the air didn't allow me to enjoy the beach, so I sat there thinking I could figure out my whole life within those two days. NOT! After staying two nights in what felt nothing like a resort, but more like a heartbreak hotel, it was time to move on with more questions and fewer answers.

After leaving Pawley's Island, I headed to Charleston to host the second Women In Ministry event through Look 'n Live

Ministries, Inc., an organization I established in 2014 while I was applying for the job I had just left. The advertising content read:

The Women in Ministry and Discernment Fellowship is a one-day empowerment event held in North Charleston, S.C., on Saturday, March 25, from 9 a.m. to 2 p.m. Women operating in Christian ministry and those discerning their calls are encouraged to attend the session led by the Rev. Dr. Arlecia Simmons. "Handling God and the World's Business" will be another topic led by Erica Russell, founder of Women With Solutions, Inc.

The efuges of becoming a pastor in Washington, D.C., didn't happen overnight; instead, it was a pastoral search process that extended from late fall 2013 through February 2015 when I was called after the first pastoral candidate did not come after being selected in May 2014. During the March 2014 Women in Ministry Fellowship, I asked the women gathered in the New Hope Missionary fellowship hall to pray for the face-to-face interview I would leave for two weeks later. The interview had to take place before Resurrection Day, which required that I leave in the middle of my 25th sorority anniversary. The sacrifices were many, but I felt God's hand was at work in the process, so I tried to trust the process. Fast forward three years later to

March 2017, where I found myself in a hotel conference room telling a smaller group of women gathered that I needed their prayers because I was in yet another transition.

I believe the mixing up in Myrtle Beach, my visit to the Heartbreak Hotel, coupled with the change of the season resulted in a brief viral illness that forced me to slow down weeks after my diggin' journey began. Forty-eight hours before the 2017 fellowship, I became ill and needed to call in reinforcement, so I didn't have to cancel the session hosted in a Holiday Inn Conference Room in North Charleston, S.C. Because my resignation indicated I planned to resign at the end of March instead of

February when I was asked to leave, I was able to maintain medical coverage until the end of March.

After a trip to Doctor's Care in Charleston, where I was prescribed antibiotics that I could barely keep down, I contacted my friend Tonetta who lived in Atlanta, and asked her to prepare to be a speaker for the session that I was slated to present. She was already planning to come and support, but now she needed to serve in a different role. She arrived in town in enough time to help me set up the room for the event. Those moments of God proving surrogates and reinforcements made me realize that grace was at work and God was not far away. One of the unexpected blessings of the evening is she brought her then 99-year-old grandmother with her. She sat and monitored our work and refused any offers to rest in the hotel room.

I'm still not sure why I thought it was essential to remain "productive" when I was emotionally wounded and now physically ailing. I had already proven that I supported women in ministry. My historic pastorate resulted in clergywomen who initially met to welcome me to the region becoming an organization that became a model for the entire denomination. There was still no reason to continue providing professional development to female clergy while I felt like a dead woman walking. How could I help others discern their next steps in ministry when I was still questioning in what capacity I would now serve God? In the mind of some, I could only represent a model for the Little Engine that could not.

Busyness is often one of the ways some respond to being wounded, and that was my response at that moment. I contacted the hotel and negotiated a price via telephone since I had already seen the room during a previous sorority event. I hired a graphic designer on Fiverr.com to make a basic flyer, and an event was in the making. The budget came out of my savings and early registrations, which were few. As with the first event, I received what I needed to pay all the expenses on the event day. With a $50 registration that included a continental breakfast and lunch, no revenue was earned, as some often suspect. Knowing I needed to stay at the hotel where the event was held, my mother graciously offered to pay for our hotel stay. Because I was still recovering from the mysterious crud, it was a welcomed blessing and made things go smoother during the day.

On March 26, 2017, one of the attendees shared the following in a Facebook post:

Greetings,

I went to a powerful women's ministry fellowship yesterday. I did not know one person in the room, but that didn't matter because we all connected like daughters of the king. I had always advocated for female clergy and a *spirit was instantly drawn to this event first because it invited women of God from every walk of life. While listening during the fellowship, I heard voices filled with wisdom that will forever change how I think about myself. I felt the warmth and spirit of all of my sisters who gathered in that service. I want to thank [Arlecia Simmons] for sharing her knowledge with me. God has truly given you a gift to unlock the mind of His believers to get them activated to work. I will continue to sit and meditate on what I learned, so that I can do all I can for my Father in Heaven. Thank you, Erica Russell for reaching out to me. I also want to add Minister Tonetta Collins to the thank you list. We are never alone, even when we think we are. I will be steadfast on my journey to reach out to many others and use my stumbling stones as stepping stones to guide others to Jesus.*

In 1 Corinthians 3:6-8, the Apostle Paul references the work that both he and Apollos had done while confronting the quarreling among the people about whose leadership they were under as followers of Christ. From Paul's summation in the chapter, we now contend, "some plant, some water, but God gives the increase." While it was hard to grasp how or why I would proceed with this activity, I finally realized that God had granted me the grace to water when I felt my soul was desolate. While I should have been seeking refuge under the covers and sobbing, God gave me the strength to take another faith walk to pour into others. It has been exciting to watch some of those attendees serve the world as ordained elders, ordained deacons (not deaconesses), licensed counselors, authors, and Christian women's organizational leaders.

The event was held with less than half of the women who attended the first event, but I was grateful that I could sing a song I learned as a Gullah Geechee child, "I dun dun, what you told me to do." But was I doing what God assigned me to do, or was I diggin' for an understanding of my ministry since I was no longer a pastor?

CHAPTER THREE
KEEP ON MOVING

April- May 2017 Itinerary

April 23: Unexpected preaching invitation in Rock Hill, S.C.

April 24: Leave Charlotte; arrive in Chicago; A.M. picks Arlecia from the airport

April 24-27: Interim Ministry Network
Fundamentals of Transitional Ministry: The Work of the Leader
The Cenacle Center, Chicago

April 27: Arrive in Chicago

May 4: Leave R.G.'s apt at noon

May 4-6: Sacred Sisters Clergywomen Retreat in North Brook, Ill.

May 6: Flight back to Charlotte at 5 p.m.

If there is any truth to the saying "that April showers bring May flowers," then the month ahead would yield an abundant harvest if the rain on Sunday, April 23, had anything to do with it. That morning when I woke up in my friend's guest room in Rock Hill, S.C., I had no clue I would be in a pulpit preaching a few hours later. Here was God's grace at work again.

A comment I made on a clergy friend's Facebook post resulted in an invitation to preach later that morning. While preaching with limited time for preparation wasn't new to me, I recall trying to convince myself that I could still minister to the waiting congregation. Because we were still in the liturgical season of Easter and this

Pentecostal congregation did not adhere to the lectionary, there was a sermon waiting in my Google Drive plump with revelation from the Lord. I remember pulling out a blue dress from my drunk collection and driving in the rain to the assignment.

While the congregation was attentive, I'm not sure if I preached in the style they may have been used to, although I was told the congregants were engaged. It was the first time I had preached for a church in this Holiness-Pentecostal tradition. I was grateful for the moment, yet I've embraced that I'm not the preacher who might make you run, jump, and leap. Nevertheless, I was grateful for their hospitality and counted it all joy. That day, they honored my service with a $200 check that I graciously accepted. God had provided.

People are often fascinated with how many people I know and the ways in which I've connected with a diverse group of souls throughout the years. During my pastorate, sorority sisters, "sista docs," relatives of friends, and people from my various stations in life would appear to support the ministry work I was doing in D.C.

One Sunday, a Caucasian couple I met during a pilgrimage to Northern Uganda wanted to surprise me, so they asked the members not to mention that they were there. And then there were a few visits from one of my male besties from Louisiana by way of Illinois, which resulted in speculation about my dating life. If only they knew, that was a whole different story that wasn't privy to church inspection.

One evening he picked me up after bible study while in town for a conference, and one of the male deacons drove up to see if we were okay as my friend stopped to calibrate the GPS of his rental car. Having friends come into town to visit was always a welcome treat, so my transition was made easier knowing I had friends in various states that I could "visit" as I searched for refuge.

Before my transition began, I lined up many events in spring that I didn't even know would transpire, given my circumstances. But in the spirit of, "if there's a will, there's a way," I carefully planned my travels and attempted to prepare for nearly two weeks of having a fixed itinerary. I'll talk more about the logistics of visiting Chicago in the next chapter. You won't understand how important that was until you've done as much mixing up as I had done and would do for the next three months.

After my friend I met at the University of Iowa in 2009 picked me up from the Chicago O'Hare International Airport, he took me to feast on mounds of chicken and waffles and other fare at a restaurant near the Catholic retreat center where I'd spend the next four days discussing how to assist a congregation during transition. Unlike the Baptist denomination of my youth, the organization I served in as pastor and others I became more familiar with in divinity school had systems in place where churches could seek the support of trained "transition ministers" after the departure of a senior pastor.

I was ready for God to take God's people back and for my body and mind to be recalibrated. However, I still had ministry gifts present, and the conference minister suggested I investigate pursuing further training as I exited this assignment. I learned two organizations credentialed transition ministers, and one would host their next training two months away in Chicago.

Already strapped for resources, I wondered if this would even be a possibility with so much uncertainty ahead. Although there were no scholarships available from the host organization, I was able to get support for the tuition, and I did my best strategic planning to accomplish the mammoth task of staying in Chicago for more than two weeks.

For nearly four days, I sat in a humble retreat center with mostly Episcopalian clergy discussing issues that could arise while transitioning a congregation. Although I had read the materials about family systems and transition, my body was there, but my mind and spirit were still trying to recalibrate. As my colleagues shared their congregational experiences, I kept thinking, "Y'all don't know the black folks I know; carry on." The case studies and cultural contexts of the places where I had worshipped wouldn't necessarily align with some of the techniques discussed. The information was good, but I'm not sure it was culturally or denominationally relevant for the systems I had navigated through as both pastor and member. I ate the ecclesial meat and spit out the bones as the primarily white male group discussed their interactions with congregants. We ate communal meals and shared our experiences, but the connections made in that space quickly faded beyond follow-up e-mails.

Although I was in the struggle of my life, Chicago would still bear the fruit of adventure. While we were advised that the neighborhood was safe for Chicago, it was advisable to watch and pray. I did both as I walked alone one night to get some authentic Chicago deep-dish pizza. I had invited other clergy on my mini-adventure, but everyone had eaten our cafeteria-style meal. I couldn't find a travel companion for my evening adventure. Since a "no" rarely stops me, I took a brisk walk in what felt like the safety of a gentrified community when I spotted a young Caucasian woman walking her dog. The distance to the restaurant was further than anticipated, and it started to rain, but I was comforted by seeing people walking and buses passing on the well-lit street. Yep, it was safe enough for me to pick up a meaty, somewhat overpriced personal pizza. I contemplated ordering a Lyft or Uber ride for my return trip, but I also wanted to stop by a drugstore I had seen a few blocks away. Although it probably wasn't the best decision I had made, I had already decided long before coming to Chicago that I couldn't allow fear to guide my every move. God was at work, and the angels were on watch.

One evening in the retreat center cafeteria, I ran into a religious leader from Chicago who was at the retreat center for a meeting. We had met a few months earlier at a conference in North Carolina, so we chatted about how I was navigating life and discussed some potential work with her organization. It wasn't hard to spot her, as few black women were in this environment. We planned to talk later, but our schedules never synched while in Chicago.

The training finally ended, and I left more confused about my future than before I arrived. During the session, I reacquainted with another clergy sister I met four years earlier when I visited the friend who initially picked me up from the airport. When I told her he was planning to pick me back up, she offered to take me to my friend's home so my male friend, who happened to be her ministerial colleague at a local church where they served, didn't have to make the trip. I was grateful for the extension of hospitality.

Years ago, one of my friends told me I lived like a baton as she listened to me recount my travels that required multiple pickups and drop-offs. Well, it was time for this baton to be passed to my clergy sister from seminary. "I know people who know people" had taken on something different as it was continually affirmed that black clergy are often connected by only two degrees of separation. You see, God's grace was seen as I connected with friends of friends that helped make the journey smoother.

As my friend's colleague dropped me off in front of the high rise where I had to wait for my friend to return home, I excitedly anticipated the second leg of the adventure. I planted myself in her lobby area and waited patiently for her return to the high rise that was once a swanky hotel in Hyde Park. I observed the architecture, people-watched, and took a quick nap until my sister came to retrieve me. She was one of the black students to welcome me on the first day of school at Duke Divinity School and provided much support since that meeting in August 2009.

Within a matter of minutes after settling in, I was headed out for an evening of live reggae music and not-so-great Jamaican food to celebrate my friend's birthday that I didn't realize was that week. Although I had no appropriate wear for the outing, I had a cute shirt that worked its magic. Applying MAC Lipglass always makes you ready for wherever you're going.

Her friends called, and we proceeded downstairs to begin our adventure, which started with riding in a circle in downtown Chicago before finally locating the restaurant near a hotel. It was hilarious. While they had all lived in the city, they were technically all transplants, and the location wasn't the most accessible place to find. After resetting multiple phone maps and speculating where we could be, we finally arrived to celebrate.

The venue featured a super crunk DJ and hype reggae band with an attractive lead singer who I later learned had quite an impressive professional background. Of course, I Googled the band after we left. I danced with the leader of the band and thought, "His breath is a little tart, but this man is fine!" On that night, it wasn't about anyone's credentials, the freshness of the oxtails, or dental habits, but it was a night of *Irie vibes,* and a celebration of a life lived for the glory of God. Although the jerk chicken was underwhelming, the impromptu gathering made my soul glad. I ended the evening with two new associates I still remain connected to via social media.

Because my friends are just as adventurous and anointed as I am, my host was on her way out of town to serve during a deliverance conference in Florida. Not only did she leave me alone in her apartment, but she also left me her car keys in case I wanted to drive. While I wasn't afraid to drive in Chicago, I was more concerned about securing a parking spot. I walked to the grocery store, a shopping complex, visited the infamous McDonald's connected to R. Kelly's abuse cases, dined out alone, and used rideshare when needed.

One day, I took a self-guided tour and ended up at the bus's final stop after traveling through South Chicago. I'm guessing the bus driver suspected from my questions that I was a tourist, so instead of kicking me off the bus when he took his break at the end of the route, he locked me on the bus where I was safe until he returned. I am grateful for the bus driver's discernment on that day because it was the end of the line, and I would have sought out some adventure the local authorities may have ended up investigating. As the elders would say, "I was free until I was fool." And thankfully, God takes care of babies and fools.

One morning while scouting out a bakery in Hyde Park, I ran into a younger female minister I had worked alongside in D.C. She was in town for a class reunion, and we were equally surprised to see each other in Chicago. We chatted and encouraged each other on our journeys, and of course, we got an "usie" of us pictured together in the crowded bakery.

God, did that just happen? Is the world that small? That moment of reconnection reminded me of God's faithfulness and that no matter where I was in space or time, I was never alone. Our worlds had collided in the nation's capital, but God allowed us to meet once again in a cafe in Chicago.

I also ventured over to the DuSable Museum of African American History, where I learned more about Mayor Harold Washington. I quickly became a conspiracy theorist thinking through the facts surrounding his death as reported by the museum and discovered via a Google search during the visit. On another day, I ventured over to the University of Chicago, where a womanist gathering was held, and I met some sister theologians I followed on social media. The public event was filled with melanated beauty, brilliance, and anointed Black Girl Magic on full display. I met new colleagues and enjoyed the free lunch offered to attendees. I caught an Uber to and from the event, so the complimentary lunch reception was a gift.

Things got a little sketchy during that trip when my rideshare driver pulled up with his girlfriend in the front seat. I prayed I wouldn't be kidnapped or arrested during a stop. Thankfully they dropped me off where I desired.

The fellowship of that day was one of the greatest gifts of the week. One of the sisters I connected with was a fellow Gullah Geechee "ooman" (woman) from Savannah, G.A., the Rev. Rosemarie Green, founding pastor of the North Shore Faith Community Church. We walked out of the venue together and quickly connected on Facebook. Two years after our meeting and connection via social media, Rev. Green became an ancestor on May 31, 2019. She was funeralized at the Second Baptist Church in Savannah on June 15, 2019. Ase' and Amen. Our meeting was special, and it was one of the moments where God's grace had met me at a table eating sandwiches and soup.

When my host returned to Chicago, I found myself riding shotgun on yet another adventure to handle business with one of her editing clients. The client was an international evangelist I had followed online, so it was exciting to meet her in person. That day, I also found myself in a megachurch that I had only physically visited via social media worship.

After that adventure, which resulted in me serving as a public relations agent, they dropped me off to get my *Teacher Appreciation Meal* that numerous restaurants gave out that day. During my pastorate, I had worked for a community college for a few months and still had my credentials. If you find yourself in food or housing insecurity, you're going to have to be strategic and monitor your e-mail for promotions that may help you out.

My visit to Chicago also yielded an unexpected opportunity to preach and an outing with a clergy couple I met years earlier. During my second week in Chicago, the friend who picked me up from the airport invited me to preach on April 30, 2017. I had never preached for a Lutheran congregation, but surprises and unexpected opportunities were common by this time on the journey. The friend I was preaching for had been United Methodist, Baptist, United Church of Christ, and now he was pastoring a Lutheran congregation.

I had no clothes for preaching, but thankfully while packing, I threw in a black sweater dress I bought on clearance and some black leggings. I was initially coming to Chicago for training and a retreat, so birthday party and preaching attire weren't a thought. Remember, I was also operating with the winter clothes I left the DMV with to begin the journey two months prior. I walked to the Marshalls near the Obamas' Chicago home, but I couldn't find any affordable "preaching shoes" for the unexpected assignment. I put on the dusty travel shoes and preached during a very spirited worship service. The couple who picked me up for service was hospitable and provided exceptional care for the guest preacher.

I tried to watch my intake but couldn't resist the appetizer of jerk ribs. The restaurant's energy, rhythmic music, laughter, and meal reminded me that blessings were still coming my way even in this season of uncertainty.

When you're navigating painful transitions, it's crucial to sit with people who can offer the specific ministry of presence your soul needs. It helps to surround yourself with spiritually mature people who can help you put things into perspective without further blurring your vision. Although we discussed ministry and church folks, it wasn't stressful. These friends understood my plight, having recently ended their tenure with a church I had preached at years earlier. My belly and heart were full, and I was ready to head home, but my friends wanted me to experience the nearby Kilwins Chocolate, Fudge, and Ice Cream Shop. After choosing some expensive delicacies we ran to the car in the rain.

The wind blew so harshly that the door to the car would not even open for me to get out. I had to force the door open with my foot and run out of the car into the building. God was certainly in the wind, as well as in the joy felt that night, as I reacquainted with friends for the first time in four years. Table fellowship was one way God's grace met me when I needed it most. Grace was more than a free meal; it was the care extended by friends who took the time to gently ask, "Now what happened?"

In the months that followed my departure from the DMV, such questions came with the territory. Thankfully, most of those meals took place with friends who cared enough about me to hold space and offer

the ministry of presence when I needed it
most.

CHAPTER FOUR
CELEBRATE GOOD TIMES

My trip to Chicago ended during the first week of May, the fifth month, representing the number for grace. In March, I was taken off the waiting list for the S.A.C.R.E.D program. Sisters Shalom Journey & Retreat. At the retreat that convened clergywomen of African descent, I ran into a sister I met while serving in D.C. and a pastor from North Carolina. She was also a Duke Divinity alumna and sorority sister. It was good seeing familiar faces and participating in sessions that focused on self-care and tools to improve and preserve both emotional and physical health.

After arranging a rideshare pick up for myself and some other attendees, I boarded my plane and returned to Charlotte, where another set of friends allowed me to leave my car.

Friends and social media followers know that May 1 officially marks the start of "Lelepalooza," the month-long celebration of my birth to two teenagers from two very different hoods. While I have yet to *LOOZA* the way I've desired, I usually find ways to enjoy a concert, outdoor event, or do something I've never done before. As my 43rd birthday approached, all I could think about was how this would be a different celebration than past years.

The previous year, members of my congregation hosted a dinner at a locally owned Italian restaurant in Silver Spring. Earlier that month, I treated myself to a Fantasia and Anthony Hamilton concert at Constitution Hall. Unfortunately, celebrating a birthday in the middle of a transition meant no one exactly knew where to send birthday cards if you hadn't given them granny's address, and the turbulence didn't yield cause for celebration. This year, there wouldn't be a beach trip that bumped up into the Black Bikers Weekend festivities in Myrtle Beach, yet Lelepalooza 2017 offered more adventure than anticipated.

After returning to Charlotte, I spent a few more days in Rock Hill before heading to Charleston for a few days on Sullivan's Island. By this time on the journey, I was trying to return to writing, so I asked a friend whose parents lived on Sullivan's Island if I could spend a few days at their home. While the retired couple went to their community empowerment jobs, I sat in their sunroom writing about the power of water. At some point, I think I took more naps than wrote sentences. The extreme temps had kept me from the beach, so I sat there thinking, hoping, wishing, dreaming, and napping. My stay ended a day earlier, but I still made time to meet a sorority sister for lunch to celebrate our upcoming birthdays.

My travels were always strategically plotted out, so we met in James Island, an area not too far from Sullivan's. I had known this sister since we were teenagers, and we were eager to meet to catch up on life and reflect on the challenges we were both currently navigating. After a lunch of Mediterranean food, we sat outside and enjoyed cookies from a nearby bakery.

As girlfriends do, we shared personal issues, such as how I was concerned about the state of my hair that hadn't been professionally done in nearly two months. Before leaving for Chicago, I opted to have my hair retwisted and styled at a cosmetology school in Rock Hill, which was a significant savings compared to going to a friend's regular natural hair salon. Before leaving for The Chi, my hair had started to unravel, but I was the queen of tuck and pin. I contacted a Chicago-based loctician I discovered on Instagram, but I was too exhausted to navigate the trip the day he offered an appointment.

When I expressed concern about the state of my locs, my lunch date paused for a second, and she explained she knew a woman who did hair out of a hotel room she lived in. By now, I have raised eyebrows, and I'm looking baffled as she sang the woman's praises and assured me that it wasn't as strange as it sounded. Within minutes, she had located the stylist's phone number. Before leaving the parking lot of the restaurant, I called the woman. After identifying myself and telling her what I needed, she noted a cancellation and that I could come immediately. I quickly drove across town and stopped at the bank to get some cash before proceeding to the one-room hotel suite where she resided with her two children. Yes, I was a tad concerned about my whereabouts, but I trusted the friend and sorority sister who made the referral. I knew she wouldn't send me into harm's way; trusting others also requires grace.

As I sat and had my locs shampooed in the kitchenette sink and retwisted, I talked with the woman who was a few years my senior. She was intelligent and knowledgeable of world affairs, so it was confusing how she could end up on the second floor of a place where transient workers and truckers found a home away from home. But who was I to question someone's living arrangements when I was essentially "living pillar to post," as my Gullah Geechee elders would describe my course? I learned that it had been a couple of years since she and her two children lived in this extended-stay hotel that was essentially not two rooms but one large room with a small couch and a queen-size bed. While there, a client knocked on the door to see when she would be available as both of her children arrived home from school. She had a phone, but I wondered if people showing up was a common occurrence.

I watched her daughter as she arrived home and wondered if the children on her school bus ever teased her about being dropped off in front of a hotel. Having grown up in an apartment complex in middle and high school, some of my classmates who lived in houses referred to some of us as "the kids from the apartments." Even as a teenager, I recognized there were the haves and the have-nots. And even if you had, there were always others who had more. I could only imagine what her children's peers had to say, as children and adults can be cruel and judgmental about how others execute survival.

"How do people end up here?" I asked myself, thinking how I could question someone else's "here" when I was essentially off to spend more nights in someone else's guest room. I did not have my own place to live, yet here I was judging how God was extending grace in someone else's life and wondering how she remained in what I deemed a temporary situation after two-plus years.

I wanted answers, but it was essentially none of my business why this dynamic and intelligent woman wouldn't choose another route. The questions I had in my mind were likely the ones she had already asked herself and didn't need anyone inquiring about again. As a rescuer who couldn't even rescue myself, I realized she didn't ask to be saved. She was not my assignment. I needed to worry about myself, and that is precisely what I did as I continued my journey to celebrate my birthday with several pit stops on the way.

The quality of her work was not impacted by her location, as no one even suspected the site where I had gotten my hair done.

Let The Good Times Roll

My locs were refreshed, and it was now time to leave Charleston and head to Columbia, S.C., to begin the celebration of Lelepalooza.

Before arriving in Columbia, my sister notified me that she had a ticket for me to attend an annual event called The Taste of Columbia, a social event and foodie's dream held in conjunction with the annual Black Expo event. After thinking through the contents of the trunk, it was clear there was nothing to wear as spring turned into summer, and this event would not be a church service, which I was prepared for, and required more than my Maxway sundresses and stretch pants.

I found some faux gold earrings and a blue rayon sundress with a gold necklace attached in a Gabe's store near my sister's house. I oiled up my feet that likely needed a pedicure, and I sashayed my happy hips to the South Carolina State Museum.

I attended the culinary event and had a refreshing time alone without anyone knowing or asking about what was going on with me. I saw a few acquaintances and enjoyed the time to take a deep breath and even dance. I connected with a friend's sister, and we sat along the wall and caught up for a few minutes before taking the obligatory "We're outchea usie" that I never posted to social media. I detected sadness in my eyes, and isn't social media only for the highs and not the lows?

In addition to the barbecue ribs, mac 'n cheese, and dipped strawberries offered by the event vendors, I enjoyed the music of Raheem Devaughn and wished they had negotiated a contract for a live band. He's the kind of singer who needs the keyboard keyboarding and the saxophone player doing her thing. I did my two-step from a corner as he sang about strong women! Yep, I felt those lyrics differently because I was in a season that required being, in the words of the gospel group The Canton Spirituals, "Stronger Than I've Ever Been."

My stay in Columbia was brief, and I proceeded to Augusta, G.A.., to attend revival at the church I previously served as an associate minister. But before leaving Columbia, I had to secure a BIRTHDAY CAKE! Read that as if Oprah is screaming it!

I mean, what kind of celebration can it be without red velvet cake and more mixing up?

One of my church sisters who couldn't house me for the night asked another family from the church if they could, and they graciously extended an invitation. I arrived early enough to catch a nap before venturing out to church, where I got to reconnect with my former pastor and church friends. I left a slice of cake with the family and headed to Atlanta the following day.

Welcome to Atlanta

After a quick stop in Lithonia to what is now my favorite, Golden Krust Jamaican restaurant, I arrived in Atlanta on the actual day of my 43rd birthday. Three of my friends had arranged to take me out to a new black-owned restaurant that featured soul food as well as live entertainment. After parking on a side street and praying the valet drivers were really valet drivers and not random car thieves, we entered the Atlanta spot where I wasn't entirely dressed for the occasion because ATL chic was on a different level. I repeated the blue dress from days earlier and gave thanks for friends who made an effort to celebrate with me during the two-hour allotted shared dining experience. I ate the soul food cuisine that was good but not great, and a guy seated next to me bought me a drink to help me LOOZA.

The live music was bangin', but by the time we were ready to get our shimmy on, our allotted dining time had ended, and we headed out and rode around town looking for a dessert bar. We ended up at an outdoor dining spot that was about to close, so we sat and talked for the remainder of the evening. It's nothing like middle age to remind you that the groove you once had isn't likely coming back.

The next day, we ended up at a cookout at my friend Yolanda's house, did a quick drive-by of the Atlanta Caribbean Festival in Central Park, and then headed out to the Atlanta Jazz Festival. While at the festival, my friend Tonetta and I gathered with a group of her associates for what became the highlight of the weekend. Libations flowed under the tent where we found refuge, but we left our group to locate something to eat. We are both true foodies!

After locating a mammoth steel drum grill with mounds of barbecue ribs, we tried to figure out how to eat a gyro and box of ribs without a chair or table. Little Miss. Sunshine Tonetta goes under this woman's tent and asks if we can stand at an adjacent table. She proceeds to say her friends have gone so we can even sit down. We sit down and begin eating, and there's BBQ and Tzatziki sauce everywhere. We're talking about what we're talking about, and the sister who is hosting us eventually joins in. She finally says, "What exactly do you do?"

"Well, that's a complicated answer," I responded before answering that I was a minister and a "Divine Content Producer." These days, you must brand and market yourself with a catchy phrase that can be used on flyers and hashtagged on social media. She began to tell me about her work and how she is a corporate event planner. We began to discuss my budding comedic ministry, and honey, she gave it to me straight-no-chaser.

She explained, "The difference between the people who get booked who aren't that good and the people who are sitting on the sidelines critiquing is that the people who got booked showed up." The woman encouraged me to get as much video as possible and grab a mic when possible. Video? (*Convo in my head: Doesn't she know I'm just working on this thing? I might have to learn this thing from YouTube. I can't go out there and make a fool of myself*).

Well, what she said to me stayed with me. "Arlecia, you just have to go out there. You might fail. But you'll learn. You'll figure it out. You always figure it out! Two days later, I booked a show that was five days away. I hadn't done anything else in two months, so I was on the fast track to getting it together.

The Atlanta celebrations didn't end with the jazz festival, but the next day was Memorial Day. Tonetta and I spent the afternoon with one of my sista docs – black women with doctoral degrees – I met in Augusta when I taught at Paine College. Her Atlanta-based family adopted me, and I had even preached at the family church. I was excited to fellowship with them, and they gladly received us. Once again, there were laughs and barbecue sauce everywhere. I even received a jar of chutney that I planned to give to a friend in D.C., one of the next stops on my journey.

CHAPTER FIVE

OOH WEE ANOTHER BLESSING

Being a planner or gifted in logistics was one skill that served me well during the season. Although I needed to make it back to D.C. before the first of June, I realized I wanted to break the trip up and not drive directly there from Atlanta. One person I needed to connect with since her husband had died was one of my senior friends back in Durham.

Miss Anne and I became friends when she came up to me after teaching a bible study about the challenges of being a single person in a congregation. During the session, I expressed how single people transplanted to a community often lack the community we expect the church to provide. While I got some strange responses after that teaching, Miss Anne took it upon herself to adopt me for the remainder of my time there. Her only daughter had died years earlier, and she realized that the problems I expressed were like what her daughter experienced while living away from home.

I called her before leaving Atlanta, and we arranged for me to stop into Durham en route to I-95. It had been some time since we had met up, but I was aware her mobility had decreased. However, that didn't stop Miss Anne from extending hospitality the way she often did during the final months of divinity school. Miss Anne, a social worker and educator by trade, had informed me that we would be rolling out to dinner. And when I say "rolling," I mean rolling. Because we would be unable to use my vehicle to go to a nearby restaurant, she used her motorized scooter to navigate her community.

The last time I saw Ms. Anne, I had visited her and her husband in a rehab facility while I was in town to preach some years earlier. Since that visit, her husband had transitioned, but we remained in touch via calls and text messages. Miss Anne is a digitally connected senior I learn something from every time I am in her presence.

When dinner was over, we crossed the road, rolled back to her home, and spent the rest of the evening talking and watching TV. I gathered my belongings and headed out for D.C. the following day. Miss Anne handed me a check for $100 and sent me on my journey with a motherly embrace. After leaving her home, Grace was present again as a free reward for a breakfast sandwich found in my Chick-fil-A app. FREE BREAKFAST! I found a restaurant around the corner from her home and headed to Interstate 40 en route to Interstate 95.

On Thursday, June 1, I left Durham and traveled to D.C. I immediately went to one of my beloved black-owned juice bars, Turning Natural. There were rituals that I began along the way and returning to this restaurant for a freshly squeezed juice, a veggie patty, and a made-to-order tossed salad was one ritual that I maintained. I called my friend whose home I was heading to see if she wanted anything before ordering, and I sat for a few minutes to enjoy the good vibes of the store.

The DMV was not short on spaces of cultural immersion. I missed some of that during my wandering season. The next day, I went to Iverson Mall and found a dress that I could wear for my comedy gig that was to be held in Silver Spring, Md., essentially down the street from where I previously lived. Before offering the comedy routine, I headed over to my storage unit to check on my belongings. As expected, it was dusty, and I couldn't make heads or tales of anything, but everything was still there.

Because it was too much of an inconvenience to drive directly back to D.C., where I was staying, I returned to my old gym, took a shower, and got dressed for my gig. The car visor always makes for the best mirror, so I did my makeup in the car. While I was able to maintain a fitness membership that allowed me privileges at gyms in a network across the country, I was glad I had already checked into the Silver Spring gym, which made it easier than the time I stopped in Richmond, Va., when I spent the night with a friend whose home was being renovated.

The folks at the Gospel Extravaganza laughed, and as fate would have it, the emcee for the program was a woman who had once written for Saturday Night Live. After the program, I wanted to know more about her background and what she thought about my comedic offering. She was shocked that the comedy thing was only something I had done publicly three times, and she noted that my timing didn't indicate that I was new to this. Her words were affirming, and we talked later about how doing some more Open Mic Nights could only perfect what I was already offering.

Later that evening, I met a girlfriend at the MGM at the National Arbor. The next day, I traveled to Bowie and met up with one of my sorority sisters and another friend from North Carolina.

While my professional life was challenging in the DMV, my personal life was filled with fun and sometimes shenanigans. The area was the first location I had landed in adulthood where I had the most engagement with longtime friends. Because the region is the host to conferences, conventions, or governmental meetings, I often saw friends, which was an aspect I missed. If only for a few days, I could get my fill of the fellowship I longed for during those months of going from place to place. Before leaving the area, I stayed in Alexandria, VA., for a few days with a graduate school friend before heading back South for the next phase of the journey.

Let's Go Down By The River

Another essential survival technique necessary during my miles of grace and transition was the weekly reorganization of my trunk, which had to store at least three seasons of clothing. My shift started near the end of winter, lasted through spring, and ended during summer.

As I drove down I-95 South somewhere in Virginia, I didn't know where my next stop would land me. I prayed and asked God to direct me to my destination of refuge. I called to chat with a mentor, and I was extended an invitation to visit her family in Conway, S.C. This is a home I have stayed in numerous times for preaching assignments, or when I've previously needed a time of respite, so I was familiar with the layout of the home and all the creatures that may be outside of this home nestled near a lake in rural South Carolina. I parked under their carport to sort and repack for my next place of refuge. My friends fed neighborhood cats because they told me they kept country mice away, so it wasn't a shock to see this one I'd seen before chilling on a table in the driveway.

I noticed an audience as I shifted my belongings from the front seat to the back seat. "Get!" I proclaimed a few times as Mr. Cat watched my every move. As I used the backseat as a folding station, the trunk remained up. Suddenly, I heard rustling in my truck. The feline who didn't mind its cat's business hopped into my trunk and retrieved a plastic bag that held my container of Lawry's seasoning salt. When the cat noticed me approaching the trunk, it ran off with my bag in its mouth. It was a viral video moment with no camera person nearby as I ran into the yard behind the feline bandit, issuing threats of "give me my bag back."

After a few minutes of running around in a circle, the cat finally dropped the bag, and I thanked God I didn't break an ankle running behind a cat. Thankfully, there are no neighbors nearby, so only the angels caught me trying to save my Lawry's.

The cat cut its eye at me and continued with its time of refuge on a nearby table. After recovering from that aerobic workout, I stood there and laughed at myself. Like this cat, I felt like I was managing multiple lives, and I wasn't quite sure if I'd make it to the proverbial nine. The pressure of all this "mixing up," as I called it, was getting to me and weighed on me heavily as I spent those days trying to sort out what was next. I would sit in my friend's garden room and ask God for the next steps. The answers never came, but I kept on the journey of refuge and making a way out of no way.

It's a Family Affair

Later in the month, I made my way back up I-95 North, but I wasn't alone this time.

One of the joys of this season was getting an opportunity to attend my oldest niece's high school graduation during the middle of the month. I finally returned to the Lowcountry of South Carolina. I met my family for the three-day adventure to Virginia, where I got to gather with the paternal side of my family, which I've previously spent the least amount of time with during the years.

One of only a handful of African-American students, my niece was stunning as she walked onto the high school football field for her commencement ceremony. Four generations of my father's family sat waving our Destiny fans featuring my niece's picture.

From my grand-aunt to two toddler nieces, everyone gathered on the football field benches to loudly celebrate this milestone. My nephew, who had graduated earlier in the summer, was also in attendance, so it was the family celebration I needed to remind me that I wasn't alone in the world and that I had the gift of a family and honestly had others to pass my legacy onto.

CHAPTER SIX
SOMETHING JUST AIN'T RIGHT

When I didn't have to worry about where I would sleep, I could consider my next steps. But I could also spend time in prayer, often one-way prayers where I asked God "Why?" every way "why" could be asked.

God's grace was often extended on the other end of unexpected phone calls. God would send opportunities that felt like they came out of nowhere. Usually, there would be silence, which required complete reliance on God. At the start of July, I got a call "out of the blue" from a churchwoman who had supported my ministry from my days in Divinity School. I had shared with her early on that I had left the DMV and was in the space of limbo. She encouraged me and assured me that all would be well. We would not talk for months, that is, until God would use her to execute the extension of grace that would help me during a rough patch on the five-month journey.

"Where are you?" she asked. "Would you be able to come to Marion and preach on Saturday morning? The pastor who was supposed to preach can't make the meeting." I had been extended an invitation to preach at a Saturday morning meeting. The woman who had the authority to invite me to the Saturday morning meeting was slated to be the lay speaker for a Women's

Day program the following day. Because she was experiencing some health challenges, she asked the women at the church if they would consider me for their service.

In an e-mail exchange confirming the latter invitation, one of the coordinators wrote: "When they asked for my opinion, I said if Dr. ------ recommended this person, she must be good. Have a safe trip, and May God continue His many blessings upon you."

Because 96 % of my wardrobe was located within my storage unit in Maryland, I had to find something to wear to these two events. Both events would take place the

Sunday after the Fourth of July, so I made my way to Charleston and decided that the one night's hotel stay extended would be used on the Saturday night before I preached the Sunday service.

I planned to leave Charleston in enough time to make the 120 miles drive, preach, stay over, and then drive to the neighboring town the following day for the Women's Day service.

But what would I wear since both events would require white apparel? While prayer and prior preparation had taken care of the sermons for these assignments, my physical body needed to be "decent and in order." Although I had my white robe rolling within me in the trunk of my car, the weight gain of the past few months wouldn't permit me to use the priestly garments for those assignments. Stuffing myself into the robe in the middle of summer would have left me looking like a Quincy's Steakhouse big fat yeast roll with an extra dollop of butter. After days of searching Ross Dress for Less and other stores I had access to, I finally found a white sundress with sleeves in Lane Bryant. Thankfully, the grace was I had a Lane Bryant credit card since 1989, so I could buy it and pay later after securing my preaching honorariums. Thankfully, it was on clearance.

The dress didn't have long sleeves, and my breasts wouldn't be covered entirely, but I figured I'd use handkerchiefs or cloth to cover what I could. I still needed another dress. The day before leaving town for my two unexpected preaching engagements, I went to my grandmother's house because surely, she and my aunt had something in their closets I could wear.

My grandmother's clothes were a tad too big, but my aunt remembered an off-white suit she was about to discard or give away. I tried to suit on and was elated when it fit. It wasn't quite white, and it was a tad larger than I needed, but it would be sufficient for the assignment. In my childhood home, I washed that suit and left it to dry so it would be ready for my adventures down Interstate 17 South, which included a few back South Carolina roads I had never explored before.

As I traveled down the two-lane highways lined with woods and an occasional house or farm, I petitioned God for more directions about my next steps. That morning, I was grateful for favorable weather as these woods were no match for a storm and what I deem my "one good eye" due to keratoconus, an eye disease that affects the structure of the cornea.

I made one stop to grab a biscuit half the way on the journey at a Hardee's in some small town. When I arrived in the town, I tried to find a gas station or restaurant where I could change into my dress. I'll never forget having to navigate a smokey parking lot, so I could get into a gas station to change into my white Lane Bryant sundress. Because I didn't know how the building where I was preaching was situated, I didn't want to risk getting there and then having to walk through those who had gathered. I finished my makeup in the car and headed to the women's gathering site.

The site was located across the street from a mill, and the church ladies dressed in their white piled out of cars in the site's parking lot. I walked in, greeted some of the women, and then announced who I was so I could get situated. It took a minute for those I encountered to figure out what to do with me. The organizer was finally located, and I was placed in an office to prepare before the program started. I began to read the program booklet for the day's events. For me, reviewing the program helps me know what to expect. Will I be up to preach within the first hour, or will I need to prepare for a more extended program?

Although I knew I replaced the speaker who was initially invited, I did not realize until I read the program that I was replacing the replacement preacher who replaced the original preacher. To be churchy about it, I was the "ram in the bush" for the "ram in the bush." My name was nowhere to be found. While I was somewhat perplexed, I had no energy to worry about that. I had a white handkerchief and white tissue stuffed in my bra to shield the flash of my cleavage. As the praise and worship music rang out, I reminded myself of my call and that I was on assignment even if my uniform wasn't deemed appropriate. I got up and began to flow with an exhortation as the worship music phased out. And then I began to pray:

"God, we thank you for this day that you have made, and for this opportunity to hear from you just one more time. Before we begin, I bind the spirit of distraction because I know my arms are out, but there's a Word from the Lord. I need You to keep the people's eyes focused on you because I came on assignment." And there was an audible sign of agreement in the room, and I was persuaded to go on in the strong name of the Lord.

That morning as I read the text and preached a sermon that I had preached in some form before, the Lord met us mightily, and tears flowed from my eyes as I ministered under the power of the Holy Spirit. We prayed and sang, and then the formal program ended before a meal.

God's grace met me once again during the repast. As I ate the soul food meal prepared for lunch, one of the participants in the program asked me about my first book, *Diggin' For Treasure: Jewels of Hope When Pressure & Time Collide*. Throughout my travels, I kept copies of the book in case there were any potential buyers along the way.

As I told her about the book and learned about her book club, I told the woman I would be interested in joining the group virtually. She went to her car and found $150 to pay me for ten copies of the book. The sale was a blessing in disguise, as it would be needed to assist me with the many bills that didn't stop, although my regular income had. During these months, the provisions from preaching, speaking, and book sales sustained me.

Grace often manifests itself in strategy and wisdom. When I talked with the organizer for the event who asked the women and the pastor if I replace her for a Women's Day program, we negotiated that instead of using the hotel room stay for Friday night, I would use the reservation for Saturday night. Thus, I would have what I needed to stay over for the program and minister in her stead.

The following day, I preached wearing my aunt's suit that she was about to donate to the Goodwill. Although I couldn't see any light out of my situation, God granted me preaching power and revelation from a deep well inside, and my preaching was more potent than it had been in the pulpit of my senior pastorate. I was given a $100 honorarium for my service.

I started to sense a turnaround at the conclusion of July. I returned to my temporary home in Rock Hill after spending the night in Columbia, S.C., to attend the second funeral of a clergy sister's father. The family had chosen to have one funeral in Maryland where the deceased had served as a pastor, and then the second funeral in Ridgeway, S.C. Before the service, I ate breakfast at a Waffle House located across the street from the Extended Stay hotel I had found at a discounted rate online.

Of course, it was too good to be true, and the smoke-free unit was smokier than my asthmatic lungs needed, but I had a schedule to keep. The hotel did have a fax machine I could use to apply for the townhouse I found in the town where my new job would begin in a few weeks.

After driving the backroads of South Carolina to get to the funeral service, I quickly realized once arriving that I had been to this church before. Like before, it was to mourn someone whose paths I had crossed on the road to becoming a minister of the Gospel, the Rev. Edward Adams.

I arrived in time to chat for a few seconds with my clergy sister, who had supported me during my pastorate.

The homegoing service was celebratory, and I was able to stay over for the traditional black family repast. Although it took a while to get served, the food was delicious. It was so delicious that I took a plate with me to Rock Hill. When I arrived at my friends' home, I bathed and went downstairs to talk with the family. I was so exhausted that I fell asleep sitting straight up in a chair, although my friends had encouraged me to go and rest several times. I attempted to go upstairs to bed around 5 a.m. when one of the family members left for a run. It was then I realized that my left leg was extremely swollen. I had never experienced significant swelling, so I just deemed it exhaustion. "You need to rest and take it easy," my friend encouraged as I complained about the heaviness of my limbs.

A few days prior, while in Charleston, I woke up at my childhood home where my grandmother called to my attention that my eye had blood in it. When I looked in the mirror, I realized that a blood vessel had broken. While I couldn't recall any trauma to my eye and didn't even think about my blood pressure, I assured my granny it was something that would pass before leaving to attend the funeral.

On the way to Columbia, I stopped in Orangeburg, S.C., where I had finally had a job offer and needed to locate housing. Bloody eye and all, I went and attempted to find a new home. While I didn't have money for a deposit, I had the money for an application and knew I had good credit. Having lived in Orangeburg before, I wasn't that hopeful about the availability of suitable housing. If God was sending me back to the "Garden City," then I would trust that God would allow me to find a place to live that was affordable, clean, and safe.

Although I wasn't feeling my best, I drove around the small town and visited a couple of rental units. Most looked like recent sites of crime scene investigations. "Is that blood or dirt?" After surveying the carpet of one unit where buzzards were feasting outside on some unknown object in the middle of the road, I asked.

After returning the keys to the realtor, I began praying and asked God to make a way. As I prayed that God would step into my housing situation, I looked to the left and saw a small sign for available townhomes. I drove a few yards and then made a U-turn to gather more information. After circling the neighborhood, I finally found a number I repeatedly called. A woman finally answered the next day, and I was able to begin the application process without even seeing the interior of the duplex. I had a good feeling about the unit, and my hunch paid off.

Although there was a good feeling about the apartment, I had faxed the application for, something was simmering in my body, and even the pending possibility of resettlement couldn't calm it down. The previous months had finally taken their toll on me. Here's an e-mail sent to friends after I spent the night in the emergency room on:

Monday, July 31, 2017:

Hello, Wonder Women with your bad selves, I know we're fierce, slayed, and our melanin is popping, but please stop long enough to pay attention to your bodies!

After a fun morning with friends on Saturday afternoon, a few lingering symptoms persisted as I tried to go about my day. Earlier in the week, a blood vessel had popped in my eye. It didn't hurt, so I ignored it since an eye doctor had previously told me they 'just happen." My vision

*returned to normal about three days later,
but I still felt a little off.*

*As I shopped for toiletries on Saturday, I
prayed and asked God for the next stops. I
finally called a friend and asked him to take
me to the ER.*

*After a few hours of tests, the doctor said I
needed to be kept for observation!
"Wha now, my 'surance doesn't kick in until
September 1!"*

*The doctor posed it as a question, but it
wasn't an option. In pure Lele fashion, I took
oil out of my purse and anointed my head as
I texted a handful of prayer warriors to pray
with me.*

*After a night of observation, I was
discharged and must now focus on
something that was never an issue: blood*

pressure! Super Woman needs to rethink how she wears her cape!

Yes, Ms. 117/78 has to regroup in year 43.

It's also possible that it's all situational as I navigate the many transitions of recent months. Either way, there's work to do! I was in the gym twice last week and eating veggies, and my system was still out of whack!

As the names of young men and women dying abruptly keep appearing on my TL, I encourage us all to take care of ourselves and not allow the costs of care to discourage us from seeking medical attention. After each needle prick, I saw my 2018 trip to South Africa disappear!

Oh, well, I got some great jokes out of the experience and brightened the night of a few medical professionals!

I was discharged Sunday afternoon!

I've been chilling for a few days. But pray for my strength as I try to chill and navigate a move and start a new position in two weeks. More later on that!

As always, continue to look and live!

The grace of friendship was amplified during the days surrounding my medical scare. In the middle of the store where I was shopping on the morning of Saturday, July 29, I called and asked a male friend what he was doing. When he indicated he was available, I asked him to meet me at my friends' home so he could take me to the emergency room in Pineville, N.C., which is outside of Charlotte. Earlier that morning, I had been on a boat with friends, but I hadn't quite recovered from what was going on after the funeral.

As requested, he picked me up, and we tried to check my blood pressure at a drugstore, and then we proceeded to the emergency room, where it didn't take long for them to begin assessing me. They took me for more testing after the initial tests didn't rule out blood clots. While my friend had left me to finish up some work, he returned, and I recall thinking how this friendship was on another level as he carried my purse and bra to the next room. "You can leave. I'll be fine," I told him a little after midnight. He was reluctant to depart, but there was nothing more he could do to assist.

The friends I was staying with were out of town, so I held off on calling them so as not to scare them. When notified, they wanted to come straight to the hospital, but I assured them I was okay and that I would see them in a few hours.

By noon the next day, my male friend came to retrieve me from the hospital and took me to get something to eat before dropping me back off at my friends' home in Rock Hill. They requested I stay with them and rest until my new chapter began.

Later that day, I drove to Walmart, secured the diuretic prescribed by the emergency room physician, and purchased a blood pressure monitor. The next day, I made a follow-up appointment with a physician I had seen years earlier in Columbia, S.C. Attempts to secure temporary insurance during the period were futile because they wanted permanent information I couldn't provide each time I called to secure coverage. Thus, I had no coverage. I told the physician I was paying out-of-pocket for the visit. While I had to pay a nominal amount for that visit, it wasn't until almost two years later that I got the bill for the remainder of the payment. Although I was responsible for the medical expense, the gift is I could afford to pay the bill when it later arrived. The total for the overnight hospital stay was around $16,000, most of which I was able to negotiate by contacting the various contractors and paying off via payment plans that lasted into 2018. One of the areas of my life that God also sustained during this season was my good credit.

CHAPTER SEVEN

LOSING TO WIN AGAIN

Although my overnight hospital observation had me thinking that I was losing ground and potentially my life, I could smell a breakthrough on the horizon. During the week of July 24, the institution where I would become a Visiting Professor had started my background check, and a nine-month teaching contract was soon to follow.

I had found a place of refuge, at least until May 15, 2018. Thankfully, that refuge wouldn't come in unfamiliar territory, but I would return to the university and town I had left in 2005 before pursuing my doctoral studies in Iowa. The location wasn't as culturally rich as the DMV, but there was a paycheck, health insurance, and retirement benefits in this place. I would no longer be a pilgrim or wanderer, but I could resettle in familiar territory and live closer to my biological family.

Although I had secured housing for my new assignment, there was one caveat: the apartment wouldn't be ready for a few days after my teaching contract started. While my sister offered me the opportunity to stay with her 45 minutes away, I remembered the energy it took to start an academic semester and decided that would be a last resort. I recall the days of coming home from work and passing out from fatigue, especially during the first days of the semester. Additionally, it had been about four years since I had taught full-time, so I now had new prayers and supplications.

Because the owner of my townhouse didn't know how many days were needed to rehab the unit, they couldn't guarantee a rush job on getting me in. Thankfully, the unit was in better condition than expected, so I had fewer days to wait. I was able to locate one AirBNB unit available for short-term rental, but when I contacted the owner, she had leased the space to traveling nurses.

As I talked with my sister about the new refuge challenges I faced, she remembered one of her friends was a native of the area and that her parents had a large home and were empty nesters. While I had only had two other occasions where I needed someone else to advocate for my housing or refuge, this would be the final and third successful time.

The parents of my sister's friend graciously agreed to allow me to stay with them for three nights to begin my semester. I arrived on Sunday evening, and they offered me dinner, and I was able to rest before my first day. My apartment would not be ready until Tuesday, and I would attempt to go and have my lights turned on during my lunch hour of that day. Although I couldn't execute that action online like other larger utility companies, grace met me because I did not have to submit a deposit. I ended my services 12 years earlier with a good payment record.

Thankfully that part of the puzzle was taken care of, but I had to pray that my belongings would arrive as scheduled. Although I could get into my unit on Tuesday, my movers couldn't bring my belongings for another two days. When I told my host couple I would be moving into my empty unit and waiting for my stuff, they quickly invited me to stay for the remainder of the week or at least until the truck arrived.

While pride was rising, I had started having some sinus issues, and the return to work had already begun to drain me. I humbly accepted their offer to continue sleeping in their very comfortable bed. I needed to rest, and I would not have been able to do that very well on the inflatable twin-size air mattress that I slept on for a month at the start of my pastorate.

As I completed this manuscript, their first grandchild is preparing to come into the world. I pray that the compassion and hospitality extended to me during those very challenging days will be extended to that child and all who are their seed.

There was only one more domestic obstacle to cross in addition to preparing four new syllabi. You know I couldn't end this journey with the smoothest process. Remember the prophetic woman I sat down with at the birthday party in January? I visited a relative's home where she was staying in Bowie, Md. While there, I ran into a younger relative of hers who owned a landscaping business. Yes, I said landscaping. Her relative was a landscaper who did whatever else was legal he could do with his truck—for example, moving items into a storage unit and moving the same furniture a few states away. The past five months had been everything but conventional, so why start making sense now?

When he agreed to move my belongings out of the storage, the next thing was figuring out how to pay him since I would be reimbursed after the move. I had to mail him the key, which I prayed would safely make it to his home in Maryland. We had a date, I had a credit card, and he had a plan to get my items moved. After a hard day's work during the first week of being on campus, I waited patiently and cleaned areas of the apartment. And then I waited some more. Finally, a few hours after we anticipated, the landscaping trailer turned moving truck pulled into my driveway with a driver and his two friends. Let's just say 98% of my belongings made it safely to my destination, and I'm still looking for a few boxes. I still haven't restained my then-new headboard that arrived with deep dents that left discolored spots on the furniture. The months discussed here had left some scratches on me, my spirit was broken, and a few things went missing along the way.

After calling the mover's mom, who had to process my credit card through her business and going to Pizza Hut to get the movers pizza and wings, I finally stood alone in my new dwelling place. I took a deep breath and gave God thanks.

When I left my apartment on February 28, 2017, I didn't know where I was going. But I made it by the grace of God and the help of angels along the way. Paul's words in

Romans 8:28 allow me to make sense of those months of diggin' for refuge: "that all things work together for good to them that love God, to them who are called according to his purpose."

EPILOGUE

Being a non-resistant recipient of grace sometimes requires vulnerability and a release of one's ego. I had to be vulnerable, as the elders would say, because "I had no pot to piss in or window to throw it out." Any pot I had was in storage, and the only windows that belonged to me were in a Corolla.

I never experienced the feeling of standing in an empty driveway because my car was on the back of a repossession truck. I never knew what it felt like for movers to remove my belongings because the bank had taken its house back. I don't know what that looks like; however, I do know what it feels and looks like to stand in the hallway of a storage unit and look at your life packed away in boxes. I looked in the $175 a month unit and surveyed the lamps, boxes of books, and containers filled with clothing that I would not wear for months. I wondered," Lord, what in the world have I done? What have you done? What are you doing?" "What are you planning to do because right through here, this is a mess?"

We work to obtain material possessions like furniture, clothing, and appliances. Still, it only takes a few financial or professional missteps for us to lose it all or to lose the place where we store all that is acquired. The grace of the experiences I have shared in these pages provided the opportunity to maintain; meaning I could still pay bills since rent and utility bills were taken out of the rotation. I depended on the refugee or housing provisions shared by others, which may have also come with meals and Wi-Fi.

The latter was essential to maintain my employment search and social media presence. I needed to log off and go and sit down somewhere, but social media provided a consistent space for me to be the Rev. Dr. Arlecia D. Simmons. Even if I felt like a fragmented mess behind the scenes, I could be digitally brilliant and relevant. There were times when I was transparent with my audience and shared glimpses of my journey, but few people ever knew about the events contained in these pages.

Some mornings when I open my eyes and utter my first "Thank ya, lawd," it still feels surreal to awake in my bed. Unlike so many women who experience housing insecurity, I was never pressured to give sexual or other favors to stay on the couches that I found. However, the emotional costs were high, and I now realize how emotionally, physically, and spiritually draining it is for the homeless or anyone navigating housing insecurity.

You can take for granted the blessing of smelling your favorite fabric softener on sheets that hold your essence. I am grateful because I can remember the days when I relied on the resources of others to sustain me. It's interesting how it requires rough patches along the road for us to sometimes identify with those who are marginalized in our society. When I look at a homeless person, I now envision the physical trauma experienced after years of sleeping on the streets and in the cold. I am also mindful of the emotional turmoil of figuring out where the next meal is coming from or where the next pillow might be found. I am beyond grateful that I had the necessary connections to sustain me and keep me safely off the street during my five months of grace.

While my experience could never compare to the stories of homeless veterans who have fought in battles abroad or unsettled women who experienced domestic violence, the aftermath feels like what could be likened to post-traumatic stress syndrome. I am no trained counselor or medical official; however, there's still a sense of uneasiness daily about the future of housing and safety.

As I recalled these pit stops and overnight stays as I began writing the book during the height of the coronavirus pandemic of 2020, I was reminded how life can change within a matter of hours or a few days. When I get into the bed with the scratched headboard, I don't take for granted that I have a bed to sleep in.

Although sheltering in place in 2020 and 2021 was burdensome, I realize there is grace in having a space to call my own. Had we been in a pandemic in 2017, it would have been challenging to shelter in place.

We often question decisions people make in life without ever walking in their shoes. Why did she quit that good job? On the outside, the job may have appeared good because it came with a title, salary, and communal prominence, while on the inside, the sister we're questioning is a ticking time bomb with health issues and meds for ailments she should not have. But she kept the job to maintain her reputation and keep her good benefits. Meanwhile, she's falling apart inside.

No matter why someone chooses to stay in a situation that no longer serves them, whether it's a marriage or a business relationship, everyone must make the best decisions for themselves and their families.

In 2020, the churchy cliches were in abundance; this is the year of "Double Vision," some proclaimed. Quickly, Christian believers and non-believers found themselves navigating a calendar year unlike any other many of us had known. As the nation shut down and mandatory stay-at-home orders were activated in many states, it became an unfamiliar wilderness period for many. It initiated a season of navigating times of grace and transition for millions across the globe.

In late January and February 2020, when mainstream media began mentioning the coronavirus, many of us listened and likely thought to ourselves as we often do with our first-world mindset, "Oh, that's over there. We're good. We have the CDC, and nothing that bad could ever happen to us."

We had just finished celebrating Valentine's Day, the great temps of spring were on the way, and summer travel was booked. Yet, we had no clue we'd celebrate Pentecost 2020 locked behind doors like first-century

Christians. In May, mothers would have flower bouquets dropped off to their porches while Father's Day cookouts were canceled as families created new ways to fellowship. Birthdays were celebrated via drive-by parades, and digital parties requiring Zoom meeting IDs became the norm.

While my transition allowed for some planning and advanced prayer, this pandemic did a quick work and forced many to reckon with our frailties, fears, independence, and interdependence on God. After completing this manuscript, I also tested positive for COVID-19 after Christmas 2021.

Like the journey shared here, there are times when we don't feel there is an end in sight. And we wonder when God will provide an itinerary or a timeline that makes more sense than the ones heard daily during news reports and White House briefings. Where is the destination, God? Where is the balm needed to heal your people? Where is our refuge in this time of trouble? These times have left many of us with more questions than answers.

When YouTube and Facebook started suggesting I view live funerals streamed by funeral homes, I realized we were in an unfamiliar place. Like me, many found themselves diggin' for refuge away from CNN's daily death toll graphic and the numerous reports. Unfortunately, we couldn't escape "the infodemic." The World Health Organization coined the term for the overload of disinformation and misinformation disseminated during the global health pandemic.

While many have lost jobs and established new businesses and services, economic and political instability remains. For the past three years, people across the globe have found themselves in some uncomfortable transitions as we have navigated the coronavirus pandemic, inflation, and rumors and threats of war.

This pandemic season has taught many Christians that our faith can't just operate on Sundays when the Hammond organ is playing, and we're feeling all tingly in Jesus. Our faith must be lived out as we remember God's promises of provision and Jesus's promise of comfort by way of the Holy Spirit. It is that comforting work of the Holy Spirit that allows us to "be anxious for nothing" while anticipating change and navigating new seasons.

Whether your faith has wavered, or you've placed trust in systems that can crumble with one U.S. Stock Market hit, remember this passage that I repeat when life feels overwhelming: "The earth is the Lord's, and the fullness thereof; the world, and they that dwell therein" (Psalm 24:1).

DIGGIN' for INTIMACY PLAYLIST

The following songs can be accessed via streaming services, or the link posted on DrLecia.com.

Alright by Ledisi

Sometimes You Gotta Lose To Win Again by Fantasia

Necessary by Fantasia (Dennis Reed)

Hold To God's Unchanging Hand, hymn

Victory by Brenda Waters

Turning Around For Me by Vashawn Mitchell

Miracles by Tonya Baker

God's Favor by Donald Lawrence with Kelly Price

The Corinthian Song by Kathy Taylor

Let Your Power Fall by James Fortune Featuring Zacardi Cortez

Movin' on by Jonathan McReynolds and Mali Music

JOURNEY THROUGH TRANSITION

You just don't need to have some conversations when going through a transition, no matter the circumstances. There are some people you should avoid having conversations with about the season you're navigating. Yes, they may have wisdom and may be well-meaning, but there are some perspectives that only someone who has been in your 8M Anne Klein pumps shares.

From February to September 2017, I was strategic about my conversations, even with family members, colleagues, and friends. I didn't need to be asked, "So what happened with you and the church?"

I appreciate the people who knew they didn't know the right words to say, so they simply smiled and checked on me via texts with minimal interrogation. They realized they had no answers, so they didn't open that can of worms. There may even be people you've trusted in the past, but their words may not be on assignment in your present or future. There's the encourager who becomes the discourager as they say what's really on their mind.

I once called a seasoned clergyman I had consulted with during some challenging times, and all he had to say was, "I'm surprised you stayed that long." While his concerns attached to this statement were valid, who wants to know that someone who professed to support you was expecting to hear that you had failed or your assignment in a season ended prematurely.

And then there's the person who shows concern but desires specific answers to their questions. I can write about what I know because I have done this myself. While being well-meaning, I have asked questions out of season and order. And the questions sometimes wouldn't end:

So where are you going to live?

So where are you going to work?

What are you going to do now?

What kind of money do you have saved up?

Meanwhile, interviewers have nothing to extend beyond rhetoric and transferred anxiety.

It's okay to establish boundaries during this season, as everyone in the pews or audience of your life won't understand or be able to journey alongside you emotionally or spiritually.

HOW TO JOURNEY ALONGSIDE PEOPLE IN TRANSITION

• Check-ins are needed but don't call or contact individuals expecting thorough reports of employment, housing, or other matters they are trying to sort out. Such interactions can become exhausting and may appear disingenuous unless you can address or meet their needs.

• Don't say uninvested common phrases like, "Call me if you need me." People who are uncalibrated can't manage another task.

• What do you have to offer? Be specific about what you can willingly extend. Friends who said, "Hey, why don't you come and stay with me for a week!" made life easier. Friends who offered meals were godsends. Oh, and please don't extend an invitation to meet for lunch or dinner and then not pay the bill. The person in need won't likely make such an invitation and may be hesitant to accept such hospitality without clarifying the payment arrangement. Come on, people.

• Please refrain from broadcasting "all you have done" to help someone experiencing a rough patch. Essentially, don't gossip about what your friend is going through, even if it's offered as a communal prayer request.

• Extend the ministry of presence and hold space when people need to lament or discuss the job interview that didn't go right. You don't have to have answers or the right words to say. Offer the appropriate facial expressions or a nod.

• When you don't know how to help someone, pray, and ask God to help you determine how and when to help!

• Avoid saying, "What you need to do is…." If they are Spirit-led, they are likely waiting for divine instructions that may not come from your mouth. Allow them to hear you through words of encouragement. You may not be the "prophetic voice" sent to correct them, but that will be revealed in due season.

• Don't judge what you do not know.

• Pray for your friend or loved one's breakthrough. Pray for their health, resources, and safety.

FINAL REFUGE REFLECTION

Months after my refugee travels, a friend texted that she found a colorful dress in the laundry room. I stopped at her North Carolina home before visiting Richmond, where I was considered for an academic position.

I recall washing clothes that had accumulated in my "trunk closet," but I was perplexed how my Maxway purchased "driving dress" could have gotten left behind. Oh, yeah, I must have arrived with the garment on, or it may have been one of the items I was air-drying as if this was my own home. In some cases, my friends' homes became my home for the hours or days I required refuge. And for that, I was grateful.

When you're driving hundreds of miles and moving as if you're on a modern-day underground railroad that is unknown to many, you don't worry about being America's Next Model. No, honey, you are concerned about comfort. Because the bulk of my travel took place during the warm summer, I blended in with my environment. There were other garments and jewelry that I would not see again after living out of my Corolla. (Years later, I am still mourning the loss of the gemstone earrings I purchased in Iowa for $100 for my birthday). But then there were intangible losses that I've never recouped. At some point along the way, there was a loss of dignity, focus, protection, and faith. Daily I wrestled with how I could keep believing although grace was steadily the wind beneath my feet.

From the outside looking in, those who knew about my situation in real-time may have suspected that I had lost my mind. I don't believe this sentiment is uncommon, as we have been socialized to suffer in silence and remain in toxic relationships because of income or status.

Sometimes, we are encouraged not to change course even when things are well, and there's a still small voice inside telling us it's time to shift, move, apply for a new job, or live the dream that keeps us awake at night or daydreaming during the day while tending someone else's field. "Just keep it moving," we are told and often tell people who chose untraveled paths.

After reading my story, I'm sure some are at a loss for words, are wondering about the parts not written about here, or have asked themselves if you could have survived such a time of wandering and unknowns? Oh, those questions may be answered later. I trust that you have survived your miles of grace, possibly taking a different route. For now, consider what you have lost along the way as you have journeyed through your transitions. Additionally, reflect on the remaining questions below.

REFLECTION QUESTIONS

1)	After reading about the author's journey, can you recall a time when a transition stretched you mentally, physically, or spiritually? Where were your places of refuge?

2)	During times of transition, what were some of the most meaningful lessons learned?

3)	If you were in a pinch, who are the family members and friends who could provide refuge without an interrogation? How would you approach them to request their assistance?

4)	If a family member or close friend had to transition, beyond prayer and the ministry of presence quickly, what resources could you extend?

5)   Extending hospitality is a Christian tenet. In what way have you given above and beyond to extend hospitality to someone in transition?

6)   How have you attempted to maintain a "merry heart" or experience joy during transitions?

7)   Do you recall a time when you have "danced in the rain" or celebrated when others expected you to lament?

8)   What steps have you previously taken to make a difficult transition smoother?

9)   As with my hospital visit that concluded the season, transitions often place us at risk or in harm's way. What risks

have you experienced due to a shift in employment, housing, or life circumstances?

10) What are the blessings you have received grace to enjoy during a transition of any kind?

READER REFLECTION

_____

_____

_____

_____

_____

_____

_____

_____

_____

READER REFLECTION

_____

_____

_____

_____

_____

_____

_____

_____

_____

READER REFLECTION

_____

_____

_____

_____

_____

_____

_____

_____

_____

READER REFLECTION

_____

_____

_____

_____

_____

_____

_____

_____

_____

READER REFLECTION

READER REFLECTION

_____

_____

_____

_____

_____

_____

_____

_____

_____

_____

READER REFLECTION

_____

_____

_____

_____

_____

_____

_____

_____

_____

_____

READER REFLECTION

_____

_____

_____

_____

_____

_____

_____

_____

_____

_____

FINAL PRAYER

God,

Thank you for your loving kindness towards me. I thank you for keeping me safe from dangers seen and unseen. You covered me as I traveled the highways and the byways, preventing accidents tire blow-outs, the Corolla never stalled, and I never ran out of gas. God, you covered me.

Thank you for friendships, connections, social capital, and the integrity that allowed people to trust me with their homes and even their cars.

I pray blessings over every home and facility that provided refuge during my 2017 transition. Please provide restful nights to all who have extended personal beds, guest rooms, couches, electricity, hot baths, Wi-Fi, meals, vehicles, and other creature comforts afforded for my safety and sanity.

Bless each friend who paid the checks for meals without knowing the challenges faced with potential food insecurity. Thank You for allowing them to be your hands on the earth when they sent unexpected CashApp and Zelle gifts. I give thanks for every unexpected invitation to preach or offer any of my skills. Thank you for comfortably resettling the elder couple from Sullivan's Island who allowed me refuge in a bedroom previously occupied by children and grandchildren. May the warmth experienced in their sunroom envelop them.

Bless every home I have occupied. May you provide continued safety and protection for every family who thought it not robbery to provide me refuge.

Thank you to every cook who surrendered their kitchens so I could prepare my own meals or allow me to extend my gift of cooking.

I pray for anyone reading this prayer who may be in a season of uncalibration, uncertainty, and flux. God, may they hear your voice about their next steps. May you grant them the strategy to walk into their next assignment with ease.

May you provide them whatever refuge they need and friends and angels along the way to keep them safe until they reach their destination.

It is in Jesus' name I pray.
Amen and Ase'

ABOUT THE AUTHOR

The Rev. Dr. Arlecia D. Simmons began her professional career as a newspaper reporter but now communicates on God's behalf as an ordained minister and an inspirational speaker and writer.

Simmons earned a Bachelor of Arts in mass communication from Winthrop University and a Master of Arts in journalism from the University of South Carolina. In December 2009, she earned a Doctor of Philosophy degree in mass communications from the University of Iowa while completing her first semester at Duke University Divinity School. She graduated from Duke in May 2012 and was ordained to Christian ministry on Pentecost Sunday, May 27, 2012. The American Baptist Churches USA endorses her ordination. Simmons enjoys educating people about the unique Gullah culture that shaped her identity.

In addition, she is a member of Delta Sigma Theta Sorority, Inc.

CONTACT THE AUTHOR

To book the Rev. Dr. Arlecia D. Simmons for speaking engagements, workshops, or writing projects, e-mail her at admin@drlecia.com. Visit her online at https://drlecia.com.

Facebook: DrLecia

Instagram: dr_lecia

LinkedIn: drarleciasimmons

Twitter: @DrLecia1

Don't forget to leave a review on Amazon!

Made in USA - Crawfordsville, IN
41391_9781736423011
03.24.2022 1013